The Royal Incorporation of Architects in Scotland

Centenary

100th Birthday Contributions from the RIAS' Honorary Fellows

Edited by Neil Baxter

Foreword

THE RIAS CENTENARY HAS BEEN vigorously celebrated in a marathon run, a golf tournament and a 100-mile bike ride. It also prompted a year-long, Scotland-wide, public-facing Festival which welcomed an audience of over 1.2 million. Its legacy will be more quietly contemplated for many years to come in the beautiful re-configuration of the little garden at the rear of the RIAS' HQ, a competition winning design by the young architect, Thomas Hamilton.

This book, published at the end of the RIAS' centenary year, results from a conversation between RIAS Secretary, Neil Baxter and Scotland's former Makar, Liz Lochhead. The upshot of their discussion was an email from Liz to the Incorporation's distinguished group of Honorary Fellows.

The RIAS' Honorary Fellows represent the creative, business, legal and political life of Scotland, marking the hugely significant contribution of key individuals to our little nation. The Incorporation has also celebrated the endeavour of some of the world's greatest architects by awarding them its Honorary Fellowship.

This volume, therefore, brings together the words, wisdom and creativity of 50 lawyers, artists, writers, politicians, historians, musicians, one priest, one planner and one landscape architect, alongside ten architects from our international forum, in a unique wee birthday card to the RIAS. Please marvel as I did at the breadth of achievement represented in the CVs of these 50 self-selected contributors and enjoy their wisdom and creativity – you might even be encouraged to hum a little tune!

Iain Connelly PPRIAS
Chair, RIAS Centenary
December 2016

Contents

Sir Robert Rowand Anderson 1834-1921

Founder and First President of the RIAS

Introduction

The decision by RIAS Council to mark the Incorporation's centenary with a year-long, Scotland-wide, public facing Festival reflects the spirit in which the organisation was founded. At their meeting on 2nd November 1916, the Incorporation's founding fathers, led by Sir Robert Rowand Anderson, established an "incorporation", not an institute. They sought to create an organisation which would represent all of the architects of Scotland. Although headquartered in Edinburgh (in a townhouse gifted in Anderson's Will) the RIAS still 'incorporates' six area Chapters, Aberdeen, Dundee, Edinburgh, Glasgow, Inverness and Stirling, upon whom it relies for much of its endeavours.

From its earliest days, the Royal Incorporation sought to promote the public benefits of architecture, recognising the unique contribution of Scotland to what Frank Lloyd Wright called "the mother art".

The persuasiveness of Scotland's former Makar, the brilliant playwright and poet, Liz Lochhead, has much to do with the quality to be found within this slim volume. Around one third of the Incorporation's Honorary Fellows rose to the challenge she set – to submit one creative page - a rich and varied response indeed!

As some of these contributions reflect, the Royal Incorporation's first century was not without its tribulations. By the end of the 1970s, the organisation was fairly moribund and seemed destined not even to see its three score and ten. The arrival of the late Charles McKean Hon FRIAS started a process of revitalisation which, happily, has continued ever since.

As an Honorary Fellow (the only Secretary to date to be thus honoured during his/her tenure - with which I am particularly chuffed) I could have produced a little ditty and included it amongst the ranks of this alphabetically ordered collection of riches. However, that seemed a little too self-serving for the Incorporation's Secretary so I have restricted myself to a sincere thank you to Charles for getting me involved (I made a point of thanking him in person while he was still around) and to telling you the story.

My own involvement with the RIAS began with a phone call to Charles in 1981. The fact that he took a call from an, admittedly persistent, student of art history was typical of the man. Busy as he was, he was always both curious and kindly.

It rapidly became apparent however that Charles intended this to be as brief a telephone conversation as politeness would allow. That was until my mention of Miss Margaret Brodie in connection with the Glasgow Empire Exhibition, the subject of my enquiry to him. He was amazed that the, ever modest, Miss Brodie had anything to do with Thomas Tait's greatest endeavour, the brilliant 1938 Exhibition which attracted the world to Glasgow in the year before the outbreak of war.

"But Margaret Brodie is a friend of my Mum and Dad" he commented. My riposte was she was also site architect for the whole Exhibition, managing a workforce which, at peak, numbered over 10,000 and delivering over 150 buildings, the largest of which covered five acres and the tallest of which, Tait's Tower, rose 300 feet high atop the 150 foot high Bellahouston Hill. "Perhaps you could come and see me." Charles suggested. The rest, as they say...

Neil Baxter Hon FRIAS
Secretary & Treasurer

Charles Anderson Hon FRIAS

CHARLES ANDERSON, ONE OF SCOTLAND'S most successful sculptors, studied drawing and painting at Glasgow School of Art under David Donaldson. He won the Chalmers Bursary from RSA the following year.

Following five years teaching art he worked as a professional mural painter and sculptor for the next 30 years for local authorities, developers, banks and insurance companies.

His most prestigious commission is the national competition winning, 1996 bronze figurative group "The Community" for Livingston New Town. In 1997 he returned to easel painting.

In 2004 Charles was elected to the Royal Society of Painters in Watercolours and from 2006 to early 2009 was President of the Glasgow Art Club.

"My painting entitled 'Shetland Moonrise' was inspired by a visit to the Shetland Isles and partly by a poem of Louis MacNeice, 'Western landscape'. Although the poet was talking about Ireland it could apply also to the landscape of the Scottish Hebrides or indeed Shetland.

For the western climate is Lethe,
The smoky taste of cooking on turf is lotus,
There are affirmation and abnegation together
From the broken bog with its veins of amber water,
From the distant headland, a sphinx's fist, that barely grips the sea, ...

... O relevance of cloud and rock –
If such could be our permanence!"

Peter Anderson Hon FRIAS

PETER IS A SOLICITOR ADVOCATE with over 40 years' experience, specialising in complex and high value personal injury claims. Major cases include the litigation which followed the Lockerbie disaster.

Peter continues to work on cases for architects, solicitors, Counsel, accountants, financial advisers, surveyors, engineers, insurance brokers, IT consultants and insurers. He was recently appointed Chair of the pro bono legal service organisers, LawWorks Scotland. As Sheriff he has presided over a wide range of civil and criminal cases.

Peter has been lauded by Chambers 2016, as a Senior Statesman and recognised by the Legal 500. He serves as a panel solicitor for the Law Society of Scotland and for many years has been a diligent and supportive legal counsel to the Royal Incorporation.

"Architects are divisive. They love to be crowd pleasers. Architects are friends of princes and enemies of the people; or architects are friends of the people and enemies of princes. Architects have profile, even a vanity greater than almost any other because they make their mark not just for the immediate consumer but for all who may see. Stand and gaze you who would pass by. Express your reaction. Everyone's a critic.

Architects are artists – who may lose their gentleness in creativity while administering works and in the pursuit of fees. They should not be allowed out alone. And that is why RIAS has been essential to fight for artistic integrity, for the higher good of all of us, and the member under threat. To protect all of the internal contradictions, the spiky or rugged individuality or pleasing conformity of the architect, which is unmissable in its mark on society at large, our public existence and in our quiet personal living. May they always exist and may the cultural richness of RIAS continue to protect and support. Architects are rarely criminals, even if they sometimes have a bad press – but they do need protectors and protected. That is where the rest of us come in, and how RIAS serves its members, and all of us."

Angela Brady PPRIBA OBE Hon FRIAS

ANGELA BRADY GRADUATED FROM DIT Dublin in 1981 and set up Brady Mallalieu Architects with Robin Mallalieu in 1987 in London. The practice specialises in housing and community based projects.

She was elected president of RIBA 2011 – 2013 and during that time had an excellent relationship with the RIAS in championing and campaigning for better architecture.

Angela brings architecture to the public as a TV broadcaster who enjoys the challenge of promoting good design to show how it changes people's lives for the better. She regards her honorary membership of the RIAS as a great honour.

" As RIAS celebrates its Centenary –
How can we work together to shape our changing world?

1916 was an important year around the world
What have we learned in a hundred years of city design,
architecture and planning and working together?
In 2016 we live in very different times in a fast changing world
incomprehensible to have foreseen 100 years ago.

'Unfamiliar City'

We now live in an 'age of anxiety' – from the politics of capitalism to severe housing shortages
and severe affects of climate change – but can architects take on the responsibility to actively
change current trends to protect and save our build environment – pushing the boundaries for new
technology in energy to new housing models, so that in a hundred years we will have done the right
thing? In coming together we can make change – just like our RIAS did in 1916.

May the next 100 years be of collaboration with like minded souls.

George Burnet Hon FRIAS

BORN IN 1927, GEORGE BURNET was educated at The Edinburgh Academy and Lincoln College, Oxford. He was appointed WS in 1954 and from 1956 until 1990 was a partner of Murray, Beith and Murray.

George has served variously as a Midlothian County Councillor, an Elder of the Church of Scotland, Convenor of the Church of Scotland General Finance Committee, Secretary of the Scottish Building Contract Committee, Secretary and Treasurer of The Royal Incorporation of Architects in Scotland, Chairman of the Life Association of Scotland, Lord-Lieutenant of Midlothian, a Justice of the Peace and a Captain in The Royal Company of Archers (the Queen's Bodyguard for Scotland).

"My family's connection with the architectural profession and hence the RIAS actually starts, long before the RIAS itself was founded in 1916, with my great grandfather, John Burnet a well-known and distinguished Glasgow architect who was one of the founders of the Institute of Architects in 1840.

He had a son Sir John James Burnet one of the leading architects of his day, and the winner of an RIBA Gold medal who following in the footsepts of his close friend Sir Robert Rowand Anderson became in 1917 the second President of the RIAS. Busts of these two Presidents stand on the staircase of 15 Rutland Square to this day.

Architecture had therefore been much in my genes, so the opportunity to become the Secretary and Treasurer of the RIAS in 1962 was too good to miss. The late Tom Cordiner was then President and he taught me a great deal about the profession. The RIAS itself at that time did not offer technical or professional advice to its members – this came when needed through the six Chapters – and it was in effect "a gentlemen's club" where architects foregathered to socialise with their friends.

This all changed dramatically when in 1964 the Ministry of Public Buildings and Works (as it was then called) invited the RIAS to take the initiative in setting up a committee to produce a Standard form of Building Contract for use in Scotland. It was to be based on the existing English document, so that, for the first time, the same contract was in use on both sides of the border. With the publication of the Scottish Contract in 1966 the RIAS became a centre for advice, not only for architects but for surveyors, lawyers, intending clients and others, I am quite certain that my Secretaryship of the RIAS opened the door to a world which I would otherwise never have known.

The late Sinclair Gauldie was a President whose friendship and advice I much valued but from the whole profession I knew nothing but support and cooperation. When I retired as Legal Advisor to the RIAS in 1992, after thirty happy and fascinating years, I was immensely honoured to be made an Honorary Fellow, a distinction which I very much value and consider myself very fortunate to have received."

Dr Santiago Calatrava Hon FRIAS

ARCHITECT, ARTIST AND ENGINEER Santiago Calatrava was born in 1951 in Valencia, Spain. He opened his first office in Zurich in 1981. The Bach de Roda Bridge, Barcelona established his international reputation. He opened a second office in Paris. His early 1990s City of Arts and Sciences, Valencia is now the most visited cultural complex in Spain.

In 2004, Calatrava opened his New York office. He has worked in Argentina, Belgium, England, Greece, Holland, Israel, Norway, Spain, Switzerland and USA and is currently developing projects in Belgium, Brazil, China, Italy, Qatar and USA.

With numerous international prizes and awards, Santiago was cited in 2005 as one of Time Magazine's 100 most influential people. Guest lecturer at many of the world's most prestigious universities, he has received over 20 honorary doctorates.

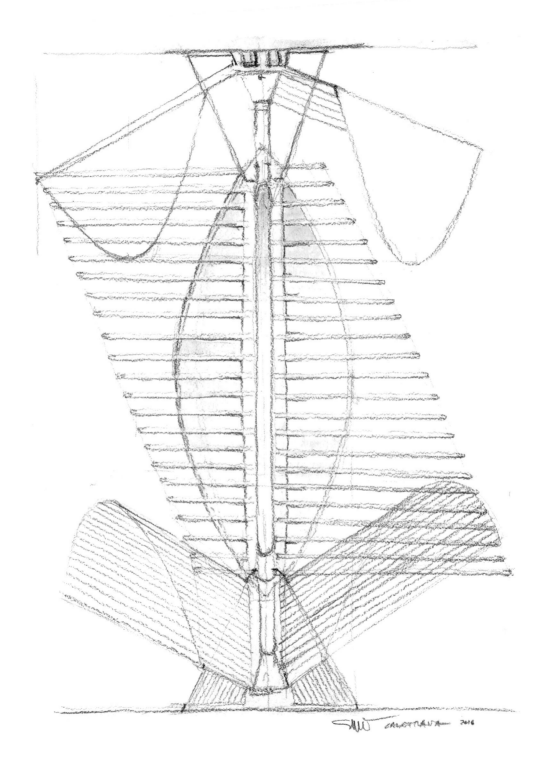

Sir Kenneth Calman Hon FRIAS

'KEN' CALMAN IS CHANCELLOR OF the University of Glasgow. He became Professor of Oncology in 1974. In 1989 he was appointed Chief Medical Officer (CMO) for Scotland then CMO England in 1991. He was on the Executive Board of the World Health Organisation. He chaired the Commission on Scottish Devolution (2008-9), the National Trust for Scotland (2010-15) and was Deputy Chair of the British Library until 2015. Ken Calman has published over ten books, his most recent being *A Doctor's Line. Poems and Prescriptions in Health and Healing*. He was appointed Chair of the National Library of Scotland in October 2016.

" Many years ago when I was at school, I wanted to be an architect. Mainly, I suppose because Charles Rennie MacIntosh had been a pupil there. But I changed and became interested in the architecture of the body. However, I have always maintained an interest, and, in particular, in the relevance of architecture to healing, in clinical settings. This wee poem sets out some of my thoughts. "

Architecture and Healing

The practice of Architecture is real
With buildings you can touch and feel
These bring to us form and space
And to all of us a sense of place
  Architecture matters to all our lives

Architecture can influence healing
To body, mind and soul appealing
Those hospitals, surgeries, clinics which arise
Need careful planning and to be pleasant to the eyes
  Architecture can help us all

The evidence suggests that Healing is best,
In buildings which are designed as places of rest
Peace to think and reflect, in times of strife
And to meditate on well-being and quality of life
  We can all feel better

Not crowded clinics, with no privacy about
And no confidentiality as names are read out
How space is used, the role of the arts
A place of tranquillity and of mending hearts
  Dignity is essential

These "Castles of Healing", no matter where
Are vital to us all to assist in patient care
They are so important to staff who work with passion
To improve the outcome with care and compassion
  A special thanks to our architects.

Ian Stuart Campbell Hon FRIAS

EDINBURGH-BASED ARTIST Ian Stuart Campbell studied at Glasgow School of Art, the Mackintosh School of Architecture and Glasgow University. Stuart's current project The Architectural Tourist involves 'rough' sketching on-site throughout Europe and Scandinavia, noting architectural "Impressions of..." which are now published widely, including in the RIAS *Quarterly*.

As Secretary of the Scottish Society of Architect Artists and a Fellow of the Society of Architectural Illustration, Stuart is keenly aware of the value of visual arts in communicating and developing design ideas. He actively promotes and encourages architects to maintain and refresh their skills in all the arts.

Warm centennial felicitation,
Mother of All Arts, on restoration.
as fulcrum to our Scottish nation.

Ian Stuart Campbell

Richard Carr Hon FRIAS

BORN IN LETCHWORTH IN 1935, after national service Richard read politics, philosophy and economics at St Catherine's, Oxford. In 1960, he joined the *Oxford Mail* as sub editor, art and film critic. He became features editor of *Design* magazine in London. In 1969, he turned freelance, became *The Guardian*'s design correspondent, worked for leading design consultancies and researched Jack Pritchard, Isokon and Sottsass.

In 1976, Richard became the Design Historian of Duncan of Jordanstone College in Dundee. He continued writing for *The Herald, The Scotsman, Building Design, Studio International* and other journals and worked with Inhouse on their Edinburgh Festival exhibitions from 1983-2007.

" Notes from a Journalist's Diary

1978

My first visit to the RIAS HQ in Rutland Square. Find it in a parlous state and almost derelict.

1979

Larry Rolland becomes President of the RIAS. Sees problems including apathy among its members and lack of interest by the public. Appoints Charles McKean as its Secretary. McKean determines to make better use of the HQ by holding exhibitions there, the first being called *A Roof Over Your Head*. The magazine *Prospect* founded and a Grand Meet of Scotland's architectural Chapters held in Rutland Square - the first for over 20 years. Also, reinvigoration of architectural services dealing with architectural law, insurance and accountancy, and architectural education, begun.

1985

RIAS opens gallery and bookshop proposed by Charles McKean six years ago. Then, there were also proposals to sell its building, which had a derelict attic, a basement that had not been used for a decade or more, and a first floor that was covered in dust. There were only three members of staff. This has now risen to six full-time members plus a number of part-timers. In 1979, McKean had set two priorities: first, self-respect for Scottish architects; and second, the regeneration of the RIAS as a learned society. These involved the promotion of Scottish architectural practices and the development of architectural services. The RIAS' collection of architectural drawings had been increased from 400 in 1979 to over 4,000, many of them belonging to the 1960s. Scottish practices numbered between 490-500 and of individual members, some 2,400 belonged to both the RIAS and RIBA, and 300 to the RIAS only. Income had risen from from £30,000 pa in 1979 to £65,000 in 1985.

1986

Princes Square opens. An 1840s tobacco warehouse off Buchanan Street, it has been converted by the Hugh Martin Partnership into an up-market, 5-storey, 10,450 sq m shopping centre whose central square has now been covered by a glass and vaulted roof. There are shops and restaurants on several floors, and the space under the atrium can be used for concerts and other events. A joint convention between the RIAS and RIBA is held in Glasgow that celebrates the building and also includes a night-time procession from Glasgow's cathedral to the necropolis, where a lightweight and illuminated model of the cathedral is launched into the night sky. The RIAS is determined to show that its conventions are far superior to those held by the RIBA. There is no doubt that this is a wonderfully imaginative and memorable occasion!

Congratulations, RIAS, on reaching your 100th anniversary - and long may you thrive! "

Patricia Chalmers MBE Hon FRIAS

PATRICIA (PAT) CHALMERS IS A longstanding champion for Glasgow and Scotland's historic environment. A dedicated public servant, Justice of the Peace and Councillor, she was Convenor of Planning at Glasgow City Council at a pivotal time, advocating the need to preserve the City's built legacy.

It was a natural progression for Pat to serve on the Board of Glasgow Building Preservation Trust as Chair and Vice Chair for many years. She combined this with her Council responsibilities and other voluntary positions, notably the Historic Buildings Council. In her retirement, she continues to sit on GBPT's board and champion the regeneration of Glasgow.

"The built heritage movement in Scotland owes much to the civic mindedness of two families: the Maxwells of Pollok and Crichton-Stuarts of Bute. However the growing need for local government to carry a responsibility for our built heritage was demonstrated by Harry Smith and his work at New Lanark. Harry then became the first dedicated member of local government to serve on the Historic Buildings Council.

The heritage movement has worked across party political lines. As a Labour Councillor, I was Convenor of Planning at Glasgow City Council (astonishingly, I was the first woman to hold this role in a major local authority) I instituted and prioritised new policies on the preservation of historic buildings. I was nominated by John McKay, former Conservative Secretary of State from Scotland to join the Historic Buildings Council and subsequently trusted by Malcolm Rifkind to sit on this highly influential body.

At a time when local authorities were struggling with many fine donated buildings, a testament of previous generation's sense of duty to community and country, I became the Chair of the Historic Buildings Council, the first woman and first pleb in this role!

I have had the privilege of being part of the development of the built heritage movement as it transitioned from patrons to the public. This is demonstrated by the ethos of Glasgow Building Preservation Trust, which pioneered the model of a project based building preservation trust in the UK. Since its inception in 1983, GBPT has enjoyed links to the RIAS. This is being carried forward vigorously under the stewardship of Neil Baxter."

Dr Malcolm Cooper Hon FRIAS

MALCOLM TRAINED AS A field archaeologist, subsequently developing a strong interest in historic buildings and landscapes. He joined English Heritage as an Inspector of ancient monuments, subsequently directing a number of their regional teams. This included managing English Heritage's London historic property portfolio including Robert Adam's Kenwood House, Henry VIII's boyhood home at Eltham Palace, and Charles Darwin's home, Down House.

In 2005 Malcolm took up the post of Chief Inspector at Historic Scotland, leaving in 2010 to set up his own historic environment consultancy. In 2016 he completed his doctoral thesis on the early preservation movement in Edinburgh.

" Past, Present, Future

The end of the nineteenth century saw heated debates about the relationship between architecture, painting and sculpture with the belief in some quarters that architecture was the superior discipline or 'Mistress Art'! Equally heated was the debate over the role of the historical and theoretical study for students. For some this encouraged a traditional and derivative approach, stifling creativity. Nonetheless, from the eighteenth century onwards there has been a growing recognition that Scottish architecture had its own history, form and identity. This was to be a crucial part of the rediscovery of the Scottish people's national identity. Four key publications trace this story.

North Britain contains every sort of ancient monument usually found in the South, with the addition of some peculiar to itself.

Francis Grose, *The Antiquities of Scotland*, 1797

Scotland has been invariably described as a poverty-stricken field as regards architectural illustration; and the writer, when he commenced his labours as a stranger to the country, of course shared in the general opinion. But he was speedily undeceived...

Robert. W. Billings, *The Baronial and Ecclesiastical Antiquities of Scotland*, 1852

The following pages ... show that Scotland contains a most complete and almost unexplored series of domestic structures, exhibiting as well the gradual progress of Architecture from an early and rude epoch to more modern and refined times, as the growth of our national life and manners.... The neglect with which they are generally treated probably arises, to some extent, from their bearing on the architectural and national history of Scotland not being sufficiently understood and appreciated.

David Macgibbon and Thomas Ross, *The Castellated and Domestic Architecture of Scotland*, 1887

Some attention has in past years been bestowed upon the Domestic Architecture of this country... Billings' ... gives a series of splendid drawings which illustrate many of the buildings included in this volume, and Messrs M'Gibbon and Ross monumental work... covers the whole period also. It is not intended, however, that this volume should be anything more than supplementary to these works. If any excuse is required from the issuing of a further volume, it might be pointed out that these treatises do not cover the whole ground, in fact it is not overstating the case to say that the Architecture of Scotland has in the past not been illustrated in a manner worthy of it.

James Gillespie, *Details of Scottish Domestic Architecture*, Edinburgh Architectural Association, 1922

James Gillespie also reflected the debt felt by Scottish architects and architecture, past and present, to one key figure:

To the late Sir Robert Rowand Anderson, LL.D., Edinburgh, is due the conception of this volume, and his generous aid and advice enabled the work to be completed in a worthy manner. "

Edward Cullinan CBE Hon FRIAS

BORN ON THE 17TH JULY 1931, Ted Cullinan, along with many thousands of other children, was shipped off to Canada from 1940-43. After the war, he attended Ampleforth College, Cambridge University, the Architectural Association and Berkley in California. He subsequently worked for Denys Lasdun, notably on the student residences for the University of East Anglia.

Cullinan's own practice, founded in 1959, has a strong reputation for sustainability and the use of natural materials. He contends that "all that educational and inspirational effort served to turn me into an architect, which I've been for sixty years." He retains his love for drawing and still draws passionately.

Tam Dalyell Hon FRIAS

After studies at Eton and Kings College Cambridge, Tam took a postgraduate teaching qualification. He taught both in Bo'ness High School and the school-ship *Dunera*, before becoming a Labour MP. He was MP for West Lothian between 1962 and 2005.

Dalyell served on and chaired numerous committees, becoming Father of the House of Commons (2001-2005). He famously held Margaret Thatcher to account over the sinking of the Argentine warship *Belgrano* and posed the famous conundrum now generally referred to as the 'West Lothian Question'.

He is a Fellow of the Royal Society of Edinburgh (FRSE), was Rector of Edinburgh University 2003-2006 and wrote a weekly column for *New Scientist* from 1967-2005.

Truth to tell, my first contact with RIAS could hardly have been more acrimonious.

In June 1962, supported by a group of "Black Bitch" Linlithgow constituents, I went to Jack McLay, later Viscount Muirshiel, himself a distinguished Conservationist, Secretary of State for Scotland to complain about the "monstrosities" proposed for the North Side of Linlithgow High Street. "But RIAS told me your lot are wrong, and they are getting a Saltire Award." End of story. What is incontrovertible is that RIAS exercised huge influence over the Scottish Office, mostly benign, in the time of McLay, Michael Noble, Willie Ross and Gordon Campbell.

Patrick Doyle Hon FRIAS

PATRICK DOYLE WAS CLASSICALLY trained at the RSAMD where he is now a Fellow. He has composed over 50 international feature films, including *Harry Potter and the Goblet of Fire*, *Gosford Park*, *Sense and Sensibility*, *Carlitos's Way*, *A Little Princess*, *Thor*, *Brave*, *Cinderella* and most recently *Whisky Galore*. He has collaborated with some of the most acclaimed directors in the world, such as Brian De Palma, Alfonso Cuaròn, Ang Lee, Mike Newell, Robert Altman and Kenneth Branagh.

Patrick has received two Oscars, two Golden Globes, two Cesars and a Bafta nomination, the Ivor Novello Award and a Scottish Bafta lifetime achievement award.

This air is dedicated to Edith Ferguson
who was my piano and singing
teacher but more importantly
my lifelong friend and mentor

Patrick Doyle.

John Dunbar OBE Hon FRIAS

JOHN G. DUNBAR WAS BORN in 1930 in London and was educated at Balliol College, Oxford. He was Secretary of the Royal Commission on the Ancient and Historical Monuments of Scotland 1978-90. He is author of various books and articles on (mainly) the historic architecture of Scotland, including *Scottish Royal Palaces: The Architecture of the Royal Residences during the Late Medieval and Early Renaissance Periods* and was co-author, with Richard Fawcett and Kitty Cruft of the *Buildings of Scotland* series, Borders edition.

He is a member of the Society of Antiquaries of London, Society of Antiquaries of Scotland and the National Trust for Scotland. He received the Order of the British Empire in 1999.

" A Toast

As a mere architectural historian I feel better qualified to comment on past than on present or future events. So, as well as congratulating the RIAS on completing its first century (and thanking it for electing me an Honorary Fellow), I would ask you to drink a toast to our forebears.

Many of these would not have called themselves architects, for this term does not seem to have been used in Scotland before about the end of the 16th century. But the very wide range of titles attached to the profession in the past gives us some idea of their backgrounds, as also of their duties and responsibilities. The early records speak of master masons, master wrights, masters of works, masters of fabric, overseers, devisors, surveyors and so on.

From about the 12th century onwards, employing theories and techniques first articulated in classical times, these pioneers of the profession began to furnish Scotland with its stock of what we now call historic buildings, some of world class and nearly all making a positive contribution to the distinctive character of our townscape and countryside.

Ladies and Gentlemen, please raise a glass to our colleagues of earlier years. "

Christophe Egret Hon FRIAS

CHRISTOPHE EGRET IS AN ARCHITECT with over 30 years experience on local and international projects. In 2004 he joined forces with urban designer David West, to create Studio Egret West, where architecture and urban design are rightfully brought together "to encourage city and building to speak to each other".

Christophe has led on the regeneration of the Park Hill community in Sheffield, the award-winning, mixed community use Library Building, Clapham, Caxton Works (mixed residential and commercial) Erith School and Millharbour Village. The practice's many award-winning projects are regularly commended for their intelligent and innovative place-making and regeneration.

Sir Terry Farrell Hon FRIAS

BORN IN SALE, CHESHIRE on 12 May 1938, Terry Farrell is a British architect and urban designer. He graduated from Newcastle University, followed by an urban planning Masters from the University of Pennsylvania in Philadelphia.

In 1965, Farrell moved to London to form a partnership with Sir Nicholas Grimshaw. In 1980 he founded Terry Farrell & Partners. He garnered a strong reputation for contextual urban design schemes, as well as exuberant works of postmodernism such as Embankment Place.

Farrell is a prominent voice in British architecture and planning. The Farrell Review of Architecture and the Built Environment, commissioned by government, offers expert guidance on the direction of British architecture.

from 'sky studies' 1990 . redrawn 2016. Joseph Hill.

Lord Norman Foster Hon FRIAS

NORMAN FOSTER IS FOUNDER and chairman of Foster + Partners, a global studio for architecture, design and engineering. Over the past five decades the practice has pioneered a sustainable approach to architecture and ecology through a wide range of work, from urban masterplans to offices, cultural buildings, airports and industrial design. Major projects include The Reichstag, Berlin and the Greater London Authority building.

Lord Foster has been awarded architecture's highest accolades, including the Pritzker Architecture Prize, the Praemium Imperiale Award for Architecture in Japan, the RIBA Royal Gold medal and the AIA Gold medal. In 1999 he was honoured with a Life Peerage.

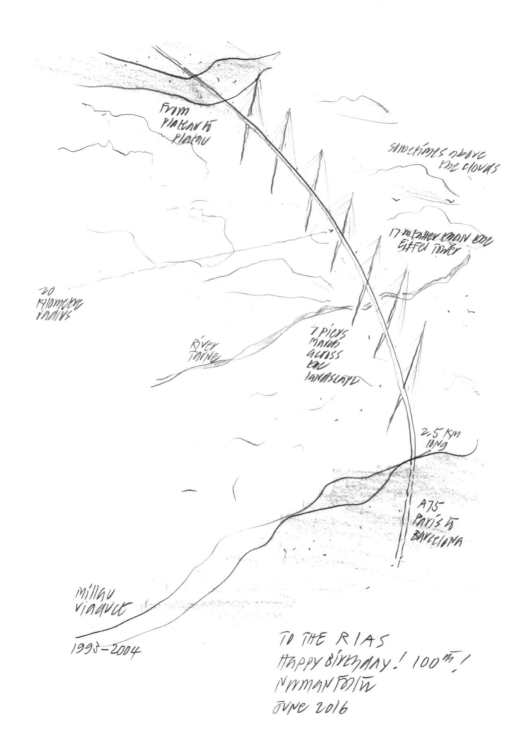

FROM PLATEAU TO PLATEAU

SOMETIMES ABOVE THE CLOUDS

17 METRES HIGHER THAN EIFFEL TOWER

20 KILOMETRE RADIUS

RIVER TARNE

7 PIERS MAKES GLASS LIKE LANDSCAPE

2,5 KM LONG

A75 PARIS TO BARCELONA

MILLAU VIADUCT

1993–2004

TO THE RIAS
HAPPY BIRTHDAY! 100th!
NORMAN FOSTER
JUNE 2016

41

Clive Gillman Hon FRIAS

CLIVE GILLMAN STUDIED FINE ART and has a background working as an artist, mainly using video and digital media technology. He was particularly involved in innovative work on the opportunities of using new media in the public realm.

He established the UK national new media arts technology resource in Liverpool in 1992. Subsequently he worked on the development of Liverpool's FACT Centre, a new arts and media centre for the city. In recent years Clive was the Director of the award winning Dundee Contemporary Arts from 2005 to 2015 and is currently the Director of Creative Industries at Creative Scotland.

One Building

In Scotland

Robin Harper Hon FRIAS

BORN IN 1940, ROBIN WAS educated at St Marylebone Grammar and Elgin Academy, Moray. After graduating from the University of Aberdeen, he taught English in Kenya and modern studies at Boroughmuir High School, Edinburgh. He was a list MSP for Lothians (1999–2011) and co-convener of the Scottish Green Party (2004–2008). Harper was the first ever elected Green parliamentarian in the United Kingdom.

Harper is a patron of many organisations including LGBT Youth Scotland and Honorary Vice-President of English-Speaking Union Scotland. Robin was Rector of the University of Edinburgh and subsequently of the University of Aberdeen. In 2008 he was appointed President of the Royal Scottish Society of Arts.

INSPIRATIONS & VALUES

ECOLOGY
Trees Beauty Plants Trees Energy
Water air Light comfort trees
Safety Old People Children
Singles families urban villages
health happiness equality TREES

PV.

heat recovery

Robin Harper Fruit shop flecir

Electric car pool

Double upper flats

Single front door older people or young families.

All north facing walls to be green walls

lower flat garden.
upper flat garden.

Water butts standard green PV
GREEN PV

school

close shops

CARS ALLOWED

WILD FLOWERS
BEES REEDS
FROGS DUCKS

BOULDERS TO PLAY ON

willow tunnel

glass perspex

Electric car pool

Tram

let nature pen the view

inner city

a new pattern of sky line

green walls everywhere

CITY SKYLINE

city sky line roof bushes trees

NETHERLANDS AMERSFOORT
A CIRCULAR TOWN
A B
C D
NO CARS

VALUES AMERSFOORT

Inspirations to architects

Meet children's needs max carbon savings + comfort your ideas of what looks good 4 Architects ABCD

Professor John Hume OBE Hon FRIAS

JOHN HUME'S EARLY CAREER was as a lecturer on economic and industrial history. He subsequently worked as an Inspector of ancient monuments and then as an Inspector of historic buildings.

From 1993 to 1999 he was Chief Inspector of Historic Buildings for Historic Scotland. He has written extensively on Scotland's industrial heritage and is a recognised authority on the subject. Since retiral, John has been deeply involved with church buildings and worked more closely with architects. He has commented that he feels very privileged to be linked so closely to such a noble profession.

Clockwise from top left:
Doorway, Whithorn Priory;
Gyles House, Pittenweem;
Tolbooth, Newmilns;
Westburn Parish Church,
Greenock; Forest Mill, Selkirk;
The King's Wark Pub, Leith;
St Peter's Episcopal Church,
Linlithgow; St George's Tron Parish
Church, Glasgow.

Charles Jencks Hon FRIAS

CHARLES JENCKS STUDIED ARCHITECTURE at Harvard and then for his PhD under Reyner Banham. He is an architectural critic, historian, cultural theorist, landscape designer and co-founder, with his late wife Maggie Keswick Jencks, of the Maggie's Cancer Care Centres.

Charles is also author of many books, including *The Language of Post-Modern Architecture, Adhocism, The Architecture of the Jumping Universe* and *The Architecture of Hope*. He has designed over 20 landscape and landart installations around the world, most recently *The Crawick Multiverse* in Scotland, 2015, commissioned by the Duke of Buccleuch.

Nathalie Regnier Kagan Hon FRIAS

BORN IN LA ROCHELLE IN 1961, Nathalie Regnier Kagan graduated from the Paris-Belleville School of Architecture in 1989. She received the Delano & Aldrich Award from the American Institute of Architects in 1990. After working with Richard Meier & Partners in New York in 1990 and Pierre Riboulet in Paris in 1991, she worked with Michel Kagan as an assistant and then associate from 1992 to his death in 2009.

Nathalie Regnier Kagan has also taught in the French national schools of architecture since 1994, and published numerous articles and books. Today she heads the office of Michel Kagan Architecture and Associates.

Michel Kagan Hon FRIAS

MICHEL KAGAN, ARCHITECT AND PROFESSOR, died, aged 56, on 27 December 2009. His RIAS Honorary Fellowship was awarded posthumously. Born in Paris in 1953, he graduated there in 1979. He received the Alberti prize in 1977.

Michel began his career in New York, combining teaching and project work. In 1986, he founded his office in France while teaching at the Geneva School, then Lilles. He received the first international award of Architecture of the Buenos Aires Biennale in 1991 and the silver medal of the Academy of Architecture in 1997. Until 2009, Michel was a professor at the Paris-Belleville School of Architecture, a government architectural consultant and a member of the Fondation Le Corbusier.

« Urban fragment »

The Châtelet-Square project contributes to the regeneration - renovation of the Châtelet area of the Rouen Heights within the «Grand Projet de Ville». It is inserted at the core of a scheme designed by urban planner Joan Busquets, with the aim to integrate new categories of housing into these social housing neighbourhoods.

Located next to a set of water towers, the Châtelet-Square project, while facing the St. Francis of Assisi square and its church, provides the neighbourhood with an urban façade. The urban regeneration was based on returning dignity to the area and also differentiating the public spaces from the private ones as in downtown. We also sought to offer housing in where the idea of «art de vivre» has its fair share. The project develops a simple vocabulary adjusted to the urban layout and generates its own identity, composed with basic shapes, easy to adapt to contemporary customs and ways of life. The different scales, and the subtly fragmented, if not split up edifices, create a humanised urban space, a vivid urban fabric full of diversity.

Site plan

Ground level plan

Client:
Habitat 76
Architect:
M. Kagan & N. Régnier-Kagan
Site:
Châtelet Square, 76000 - Rouen, France
Program:
50 social housing units,
4 activities offices, 48 parking spaces
Surface Area:
5 568 sq. m. Net Area
Cost:
7,43 M€ exclusive of taxes
Survey Date:
2007 - 2011
Completion:
2015

«Rouen Châtelet Square»
50 social housing units and activities offices

Dame Barbara Kelly Hon FRIAS

BARBARA KELLY IS CHAIRWOMAN of Dumfries and Galloway Arts Festival and, until 2013, was Convenor of the Crichton Foundation.

A former Trustee of the Royal Botanic Gardens in Edinburgh, she is also a former Trustee of the Equal Opportunities Commission, a former Board Member of Scottish Enterprise, was Chair of the Scottish Consumer Council, first Chairperson of the ARB and Chair of the Millennium Forest for Scotland. She currently Chairs the Robertson Trust.

In addition to active participation in architectural education (on the Scottish Part III Committee), other architectural involvements include her participation in the President's Commission on Procurement (2011-2012) and as a judge for the Dynamic Place Awards (founded by RIAS) and the Doolan Prize.

" Hoorah for the RIAS Centenary Year 2016

Woodcut: John O'Connor

Barncleugh Thoughts from home.

All my life I have had a passionate interest in architecture. I inherited that love from parents who, in my childhood, made certain we visited significant buildings all round the UK and beyond. To this day, I am excited by the inspiration, aesthetics, diversity and skill displayed by architects since the beginning of time. Whether for living, working or worshipping in, buildings are rarely set in aspic but reflect the needs of the people who inhabit them.

Prof Edward Hollis recently said that 'a building is a capricious thing; it is inhabited and changed, and its existence is a tale of constant and curious transformation.'

My own home was built in the late 1500s and has grown thro' the centuries to accommodate the needs of countless generations. As a consequence of the skills of the architects involved in the five hundred years of its existence, it remains a beautiful and happy place.

That is something to celebrate.

"

Neil Kelly Hon FRIAS

NEIL KELLY IS A PARTNER IN solicitors MacRoberts LLP where he is Head of the Construction Group.

Neil has been advising contractors, sub-contractors, suppliers and consultants in the construction sector for over 30 years. In addition to his RIAS Fellowship he was made an Honorary Member of the Royal Institution of Chartered Surveyors in 2007 and in 2016 given a special award by the Chartered Institute of Building.

Outside the law Neil has a keen interest in the arts, particularly opera. He sits on the Board of the Scottish Ensemble and is a past Chair of the Voices Festival held annually in St Andrews.

"Keep this quiet. I always wanted to be an architect. An architect, not a lawyer.

Le Corbusier was right. Architecture is 'the learned game ... of forms assembled in the light'.

Architecture contributes so much to the nature of the physical environment in which we all live. Lawyers not so much!

The aesthetic of a particular architect or building may sometimes divide opinion but it is very rare indeed if we don't admire at least some aspect of light, colour, space, proportion or function.

Architecture is very much a visual art but buildings can speak for themselves. In my line, for example, great buildings make great court houses.

They are a rare combination of architecture and the law. Architecture used to provide the physical embodiment of the law or a legal system.

Happy Centenary RIAS!

I look forward to the next 100 years and the many wonderful buildings your members will continue to give us."

Professor Martin Kemp Hon FRIAS

MARTIN KEMP TAUGHT AT THE universities of Glasgow and St Andrews before his 1995 appointment as Professor of the History of Art at Oxford. His publications include *The Science of Art*, *The Human Animal in Western Art and Science*, *Leonardo da Vinci. Christ to Coke*, *Art in History* and *Structural Intuitions*.

Martin has been a Trustee of the National Galleries of Scotland, The Victoria and Albert and British Museums. He has curated exhibitions including *Spectacular Bodies* at the Hayward Gallery, *Leonardo da Vinci. Experience, Experiment, Design* at the V&A and *Seduced. Sex and Art from Antiquity to Now* at the Barbican. He is a full-time speaker, writer and broadcaster.

" Kellie Castle

Kellie Castle confronts the Bass Rock across the shining waters of the Forth. It is on the land, in the land and of the land. Towers, corbels, turrets, gables - the vocabulary seems to be that of military matters. Yet the discourse is not that of war. The stony eloquence is that of the native nature of coastal Fife. The intonation of the pedimented dormers internationally evokes the Renaissance castles of the Loire. We are not dealing with a "baronial castle" – the odd term that misses what is unique about large-scale Scottish secular building in the sixteenth century. What we are seeing is a special kind of Scottish castle-palace. It declares its status as castle through rhetoric rather than credible function. A simple upright mediaeval tower served as the sire to its two later companions, the whole coming to assume a declamatory air. The shapely declamations of castle-ness are fitting for a local laird but are hardly intended to resist a mighty siege. Between the towers is the palace block, the ample rectangular windows hinting at the humane grandeur that comprises the unique character of Kellie's radiant domestic interiors.

It would be wrong, however, to treat Kellie just as a specimen of architecture, fine though it is. Kellie is infused with the family life of the Lorimers, the aura of which seeps from every pore of the fabric of the building and the haunts the sheltered nooks of the garden. The historic fabric, left more or less in its present form by Sir Thomas Erskine, the first Earl of Kellie, had fallen into abandon by the nineteenth century. It was rescued by James Lorimer, Regius Professor of Public Law at Edinburgh, and became a family home. And what a family the Lorimers proved to be! We may think most obviously of the professor's sons, the great architect Sir Robert and the brilliant if underrated painter, John Henry. The interiors are enriched by Robert's substantial furniture, and adorned with his brother's luminous canvases of Kellie, indoors and outdoors. In the next generation we readily recall Hew Lorimer, the finest

monumental sculptor of his generation in Scotland. He was above all a carver of stone. What other sculptural medium could he have adopted as a child of Kellie? It was Hew who staged a second rescue of Kellie after it had fallen into disuse in the 1930's. The professionals are the most conspicuous branches in an extended family tree of creativity in in the visual and musical arts (charted delightfully by Charlotte Lorimer: www.upward-onward.com). It was Hew who conveyed the house into the present care of the National Trust.

Visiting Kellie these days – it was my local castle for many years – we grasp that it is a house with personality. It is not the grandest castle of its type. We may think of somewhere like Fyvie or Glamis. But we can enjoy a specially human relationship with it. If we are fortunate enough to enter the understated front door, the ample and inviting staircase is impressive without being oppressive. The expansive hall on the piano nobile is infused by the domestic warmth of cherished grandparents, the busy concern of mothers and fathers and, above all, the bubbling charm of laughing children. Hew's own pesence is notably tangible, above all in the dusty stables that served as the studio in which his left hand drove his sharp chisels into the pliant stone. There can be no better reminder that architecture is about people. "

Lorraine Landels Hon FRIAS

LORRAINE IS AN ARTS AND design graduate from Edinburgh College of Art. Her early career was with Reiach and Hall in Edinburgh, on graphic and interior design and subsequently business development.

Lorraine married the late Jim Landels, a much loved member of the Incorporation, in 1978. They were keen participants in many RIAS events throughout the 1980s onwards.

After working with, among others, Tayburn and McIroy Coates in the early 2000s she became Business Development Director at Martha Schwartz Inc. For the last five years Lorraine has served as Director of Strategic Relationships at BuroHappold, now one of the world's largest engineering consultancies.

" Looking to the streets and not the skies...
and forget about chasing Pokémon

I first met Jan Gehl in the mid 1970's when I was an art student at Edinburgh College of Art. At the time I was fascinated with architecture and the new generation who were beginning to redefine architecture with a divergence in opinions – replacing the functional and formalised shapes of the modernist style in a rediscovery of past architectural ornament and forms. It was still early days and I was curious – and perhaps not convinced. Meeting Jan was timely.

Jan didn't talk a design language. He didn't talk architecture. He talked about places and people. He advised against looking at the skies, and instead, suggested we study people – or more importantly, how people interacted with each other and used our public spaces. He advocated giving the streets back to people and cars being banished from our city centres.

Jan's simple message has changed little over the years. It was evident as I walked around the Biennale this year how strong Jan's philosophy permeates today. His once singular voice has become main stream in a cacophony of thinking in the world of architecture and planning. Amongst many architects supporting Jan's mantra, Alejandro Aravena's curation of the 2016 Biennale demonstrated Jan's legacy is safe. It was reassuring walking around the Giardini and Arsenale earlier this year.

The world is a better place having Jan in it.

I met another (now) hero recently in Broken Hill, a small former mining town in the Australian Outback. Ammin-Nullah 'Robert' Shamoze, or Bob for short, was looking after a small red corrugated iron mosque. The oldest mosque in New South Wales. His father had brought the first camels to Australia from Afghanistan for the mining industry. The mosque was first built at the cameleer camp in 1891. Bob had a fascinating history himself, he wasn't raised a Muslim but, saw it his place in late life, to ensure that this gem of Australian's history was accessible to the public to remind them of Australia's recent mining history and diversity of culture – and as a place for any passing faithful to pray .

The world is full of heroes like Jan and Bob. They have something in common. They care about real people and places, their stories, and our legacy – and they don't chase Pokémon. "

Liz Lochhead Hon FRIAS

FORMERLY SCOTLAND'S MAKAR, Liz Lochhead is one of Scotland's foremost poets and dramatists.

From North Lanarkshire she attended Glasgow School of Art. One of Scotland's most popular dramatists, her plays include *Mary Queen of Scots Got Her Head Chopped Off*, *Perfect Days* and her Scots adaptation of Moliere's *Tartuffe*. Her adaptation of Euripides' *Medea* won the Saltire Scottish Book of the Year Award in 2001. Her poetry collections including *True Confessions*, *Bagpipe Muzak*, *Dreaming Frankenstein* and *The Colour of Black and White*.

Liz's marriage to the late Tom Logan, a talented and charismatic architect, reinforced an already keen interest in architecture, apparent in much of her work. As a performance artist, Liz brings an impeccable sense of timing. Her work is spiced with humour and irony, invariably as thought provoking as it is entertaining.

"Written – in its first version – for the Royal Incorporation of Architects in Scotland on the occasion of the Annual Fellows Dinner in 2012.

(And – because I work as a poet, not an architect – and therefore get to build something all over again if I like, just like that, better and more complete, I hope, saying what it should have said in the first place – rewritten in honour and celebration of this profession I admire for the RIAS Centenary Year, 2016.)"

Grace

Once in Moab
before *the land of milk and honey*
it was written in Deuteronomy
that before breaking bread together, friends, we should
take pause, and then say grace.
Which was to say we were to bless
what blessed us with everything that was good.
God — or the
land of the wheat and the barley, the
source of all our food,
the land of the vine and the fig and the pomegranate,
the land of the oil-olive and the syrup-date.

This is Scotland, this
our one small country in this great wide world, which is
our one, wondrous, spinning, dear green place.
What shall we build of it, together
in this our one small time and space?

We are far from Deuteronomy,
far from long forgotten
Moab, far from any land of milk and honey —
we are where *nothing is written*

Yet tonight
together
for good food and even better fellowship,
        whether we have a God or not
            our gratitude cannot be denied.

And we shall eat, and we shall be satisfied.

Liz Lochhead

Phyllis Logan Hon FRIAS

PHYLLIS LOGAN WAS BORN IN Paisley and brought up in Johnstone. She graduated from the RSAMD, now the Royal Conservatoire of Scotland, in the late 1970s. She spent her early working life in the theatre performing in various shows at the Traverse Theatre and touring several productions with Borderline Theatre Company.

Phyllis has appeared in television and film throughout her career. Notable roles include *Another Time, Another Place* for which she won many awards and the TV hit, *Lovejoy*. Her most recent role was playing Mrs Hughes in all six series of *Downton Abbey*.

Thank you

My talents lie not with the pen
I cannot draw nor write
My 'matchstick men' and women
Could be fairly hailed a sight.

My scribblings look like they've been penned
By a spider in a hurry
It would indeed be fair to say
Liz Lochhead need not worry.

I only speak another's words
to earn an honest crust
But now I vow to speak my own —
it's only right and just!

I'm Proud to be an Hon FRIAS
And thank you most sincerely
Your Kindness in bestowing it
Is an honour I'll hold dearly.

Congratulations on your Centenary.

Dr Anne Lorne Gillies Hon FRIAS

DR ANNE LORNE GILLIES COMBINES classical music training with a deep love and understanding of Gaelic tradition. For over 50 years her singing career has crossed borders and boundaries, and her contribution to Scottish culture is widely recognised. She has written, performed and provided extensively for television and the stage.

In 2009 Anne was named the Scottish Government's Gaelic Ambassador of the Year. In 2012 she was inducted into the Traditional Music Hall of Fame and on International Women's Day 2015, after a popular poll organised by the Saltire Society, she was named as one of ten 'Outstanding Women of Scotland'.

" A Tale of Two Buildings

In the latter part of the 18th century Gaelic-speaking asylum-seekers streamed into Glasgow, leaving large tracts of Scotland scarred irrevocably by what Sorley Maclean called "the terrible imprint of the clearances". St Columba's Gaelic Church of Scotland was born in response to their needs – spiritual, social, linguistic. In 1899, when their original premises in Hope Street were demolished to make way for the sprawl of Central Station, generous compensation from the Caledonian Railway Company enabled the building of a fine new church to an ambitious design by Tennant and Burke. It's still standing in St Vincent Street, its congregation still worshipping in Gaelic.

The inscription above the door – 'Tigh mo chridhe, Tigh mo ghràidh' (*House of my heart, House of my love*) – was carved by Duncan Livingstone (1877-1964) a stone-mason from Mull who went on to become an equally dexterous poet. Educated in Tobermory, where he and his schoolfriends were thrashed if the teacher caught them speaking Gaelic and lives were still scarred by the long shadow of the Mull potato famine, Duncan left home for the noisy city, completed his apprenticeship as a mason, and attended evening classes in Glasgow Technical College.

His life changed even more radically when, at the start of the Boer War, he crossed the world – like countless Highlanders before and since – to fight for the British Empire. Wounded in the leg, he was sent back to Glasgow, where he stayed long enough to add some finishing touches to his people's church. But he had seen enough of South Africa to appreciate the opportunities it offered a skilled stone-mason.

Before the brave new St Columba's Church had even opened its doors Duncan had left Scotland forever and emigrated to Pretoria. He did well from the start. His reputation was sealed by the prestigious appointment as Clerk of Works on the construction of the new Government's administrative centre. Designed by Herbert Baker, English colonial "architect-laureate" of his day, the Union Building rose out of the remains of a disused quarry above Pretoria, its wings joined by a colonnade symbolising unity between two divided peoples, its twin towers representing the two dominant languages of the Union, English and Afrikaans: or (to borrow a phrase from South African architect Jeremy Foster) "the transformative power of African stone subjected to European skill". Duncan's disarming panegyric

'Togalach an Aonaidh' (*The Union Building*) is written very much in "The Grand Manner":

(Bardically speaking!)
"*...Aotrom, uallach air an leathad, tha thu suidhichte ad loinn Òirdhearc thu, chaneil do leithid an leth-dheas an t-saoghail chruinn. Do chuilbh chumhachdail, glan shnaidhte, do boghachan, mar rannan dàin Sreath air shreath a' ruith gu snasmhor cumte le sàr ealadhain...*
("*...Airy, majestic, you stand on the hillside in your glory Cynosure of buildings in all the southern hemisphere. Your commanding columns, neat-hewn, your arches like poetic verses Flowing row after row, each a masterpiece in its own right...*)

Given the iniquity of the Highland Clearances, it may seem strange how little the Gaelic poets of the 18th and 19th centuries identified with victims of colonisation elsewhere. Or, indeed, how smoothly Duncan Livingstone seems to have slipped into the role of genial ex-pat – playing bowls, organising the Celtic Society, and carving Gaelic poems out of the everyday – in denial, apparently, of the harsh realities of life outwith the cocoon of white majority Pretoria.

And yet... In the early 1960s, when the apartheid state was banning political organisations and many black writers were being forced into exile, Duncan's douce Gaelic readership was astounded by the sudden appearance of a stark anti-supremacist diatribe 'Feasgar an duine ghil' (*The Twilight of the White Man*) and a heart-breaking lament 'Bean Dubh a' Caoidh a Fir a Chaidh a Mharbhadh leis a' Phoileas' (*A Black Woman Mourns her Husband Killed by the Police*) which in itself could earn him a place among champions of justice from Robert Burns to Mongane (Wally) Serote.

Duncan died twenty years before Nelson Mandela stood in the embrace of the Union Building in Pretoria, to deliver his historic inaugural speech as South Africa's first black president: "...Never again will this beautiful land experience the oppression of one by another...". If only Duncan Livingstone had been there that day – to write a panegyric, perhaps, for a great international hero, or to carve his own Gaelic inscription above the entrance of the Union Building: 'Tigh ar cridhe, Tigh ar gràidh – mu dheireadh thall.' (*House of our hearts, House of our love – at last*). "

Roy Martin Hon FRIAS

ROY MARTIN QC IS A LONG-SERVING advocate and barrister in Scotland and England. He practises largely in land and property and has particular experience of planning, environmental and compulsory purchase law. He has a reputation for sharp analysis and ready wit.

Roy is a judge of the Courts of Appeal in Jersey and Guernsey and was Dean of the Faculty of Advocates. He was one of the first Affiliates of the RIAS and has a keen interest in modern architecture. In 2011-12 he served on the RIAS President's Commission on procurement which helped to prompt the Scottish Government's construction procurement review.

" What of architecture in Scotland in the last hundred years? The innovation and imagination of the 1920s and 30s ended by war. The municipal uniformity of the 1950s and the system-built brutalism of the 1960s and 70s. The inevitable reactionary conservatism and increasing rule by regulation and planning diktat. The lowest common denominator of design by committee and unqualified official. Yet despite these factors, the increasing confidence and inspiration of the 1990s and early 21st-century. That Scotland has produced and maintains so many fine buildings, restorations and renovations against this chequered background is a credit to the RIAS and its members. Long may it continue. "

Professor Tom Maver Hon FRIAS

NOW AT THE MACKINTOSH SCHOOL, Tom Maver has been at the forefront of information technologies applied to building design since 1970. When the technology was in its infancy, he founded ABACUS (Architecture and Building Aids Computer Unit, Strathclyde) a research group within the University of Strathclyde. Under his Directorship, over the next 32 years, ABACUS built an international reputation in CAAD, MultiMedia, Virtual Reality, Urban Models and Energy Efficient Design. This reputation was recognised in the top rating of 5* (international excellence) by the UK Higher Education Funding Council and in several international lifetime achievement awards. He has also been awarded The IHVE Bronze Medal and the Gold Medal of the Royal Society.

CAAD: A Five Decade Paradigm Shift

The 1960s – how we input/output the description of buildings

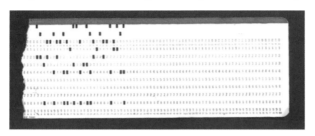

```
AAAAAAAAAAA AAAAAAAAAAA                              HHHHHHHHHHHHH
AAAAAAAAAAA AAAAAAAAAAA CC FFFFFFFFFFFFFFFFFFFHHHHHHHHHHHHHH
AAAAAAAAAAA AAAAAAAAAAA CC FFFFFFFFFFFFFFFFFFFFHHHHHHHHHHHHHH
AAAAAAAAAA CCCCCCCCCCC CC FFFFFFFFFFFFFFFFFFFFHHHHHHHHHHHHHH
CCCCCCCCCCC CCCCCCCCCCC CC CCCCCCCCCCCCCCCCCCC CCCCCCCCCCC
CCCCCCCCCCC EEEEEEEEEEEEE GGGGGGGGGGGGGGGGGGGCC DDDDDDDDDD
DDDDDDDDDDD EEEEEEEEEEEEE GGGGGGGGGGGGGGGGGGGCC DDDDDDDDDD
DDDDDDDDDDD EEEEEEEEEEEEE GGGGGGGGGGGGGGGGGGGCC DDDDDDDDDD
                         GGGGGGGGGGGGGGGGGGGCC DDDDDDDDDD
                         GGGGGGGGGGGGGGGGGGGCC DDDDDDDDDD
```

2016 – what we can do now

"… a science of design, a body of intellectually tough analytical, partly formalizable, partly empirical, teachable doctrine about the design process."

Herbert Simon, The Sciences of the Artificial, 1968

"CAAD … a great opportunity for architects to become master builders again."

Frank Gehry in his RIBA Gold Medal acceptance speech, 2003

"… this paradigm shift in architectural design, the first in 400 years, is in its infancy. Should we wish to realize its potential, we MUST allow our students to realize their ambition."

Tom Maver, Research Professor,
Mackintosh School of Architecture, 2016

2016 image provided by 10 DESIGN an international practice with offfices in Edinburgh, Hong Kong, Dubai, Shanghai

Anne McChlery Hon FRIAS

ANNE MCCHLERY HAS BEEN Director of Glasgow Building Preservation Trust (GBPT) since 2005. With an MPhil in Urban Regeneration and Dip Housing, she has a breadth of new build and historic development knowledge honed over many years working with local government, housing associations and the charitable sector.

Bringing well-honed management skills and fundraising expertise to GBPT, Anne has overseen the delivery of award-winning restorations and Glasgow's annual Doors Open Days Festival, celebrating the city's built heritage. Particular career highlights at the Trust include the restoration of Castlemilk Stables, Pollokshaws West Station, Gartnavel Chapel and Kelvingrove Bandstand.

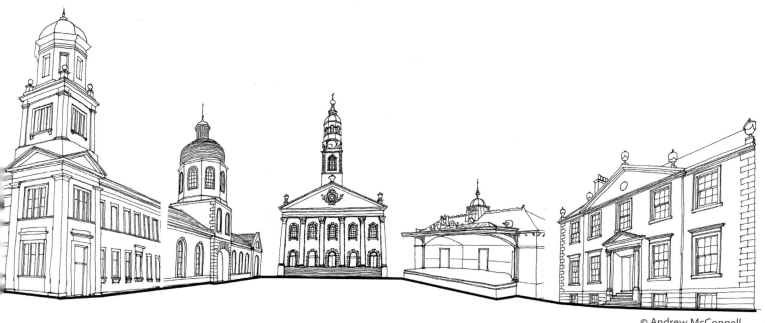

© Andrew McConnell

"Congratulations from Glasgow Building Preservation Trust to RIAS in reaching your first 100 years.

At Glasgow Building Preservation Trust we love our city and work hard to save our glorious buildings. We are determined to carry on partnering with likeminded organisations and people, bringing new life, designs and uses to old buildings. We are supported by the Heritage Lottery Fund, Glasgow City Council, Historic Environment Scotland, the Architectural Heritage Fund and many others in this challenging but rewarding endeavour.

As an Honorary Fellow I would say very well done to RIAS for bringing more women into the fold, and promoting inclusion!"

Tom McInally Hon FRIAS

TOM MCINALLY BECAME A professional town planning apprentice in the Corporation of the City of Glasgow Department of Architecture and Civic Design on the 15th August 1966.

In the fifty years since, Tom has seen many changes in planning and architecture having worked on some of the largest and most complex development projects in Scotland including the GEAR Project, Glasgow Harbour, Heartlands, Queens' Quay, and the Central Govan Action Plan. He brings unique experience of 'both sides of the argument' to much planning decision making – which may account for his reputation for delivering.

" Happy Birthday to the RIAS

The 15th of August this year marked my 50th year since stepping onto the Department of Architecture and Civic Design in Glasgow as a professional Town Planning apprentice. I feel I should take this opportunity to pay tribute to the architects who helped me understand architecture and design.

In the beginning planning apprentices had limited contact with architects but were tasked with checking the Dean of Guild applications to establish which projects needed planning consent. A few hard lessons from Bert Gauld at the Dean of Guild's office let me know where planners stood at that time in the scheme of urban development. In 1966 planning was a relatively new profession. It was clear we had a long way to go to gain respect from other professionals.

My first lessons in architecture came from day release lectures from Philip Cocker. He opened up the eyes of us students to a new understanding. A primary memory from Philip was the use of full height and width windows to bring the garden into the living room, integrating architecture and landscape.

Back in the office my education continued in regular sessions with Bob Whitten and Joe Khan who had transferred to planning from the Council's architects department. Bob had become my boss and Joe worked in the next office. I became a regular listener, hearing them discuss urban design with visiting architects promoting development proposals. I was introduced to architects from all areas of the country.

As my career developed and with increasing responsibility for the GEAR project in the East End more significant lessons came from Alex Kerr, the Senior Planner in the Scottish Office who had been a gold medal architecture student at Glasgow School of Art but who had had been attracted to planning after many years as an architect in the redevelopment areas of Glasgow and the planning of Cumbernauld New Town. Alex became a regular visitor who stimulated much thought about how planning needed to effect change rather than being simply a bureaucratic process which he felt it was in danger of becoming.

During my learning curve with Alex I also came to know Jim Fisher, Senior Partner in Scott Brownrigg and Turner, a regular visitor for meetings with Joe Khan and Bob Whitton. Jim and Alex Kerr had been students at the School of Art at the same time. I reunited them, rekindling an old friendship. Much discussion ensued between one of Scotland's most pragmatic architects and one of our most ideological. Jim was the quick witted pragmatist, skilled with the one line riposte. Alex tended to take the more holistic higher ground. The discussions between these two have been amongst the more influential of my career. I am eternally grateful. Unfortunately Jim succumbed to cancer but Alex, now approaching 90, continues to provoke in his own inimitable manner.

The lessons learned from these and other architects during my long career have enabled me to develop sound relationships and respect with many architects. I am grateful for the opportunity to thank them and offer my very best wishes to the RIAS. "

Father Dermot Morrin OP Hon FRIAS

FATHER DERMOT WAS BORN in Ireland in 1964. His father was a farmer and Dermot is the youngest of three sons. He wanted to be an architect, but then changed his mind and studied electronic engineering instead.

Later on, Dermot found himself drawn to the priesthood and was ordained in 1997. As a member of the Dominican Community at St Albert's Catholic Chaplaincy in Edinburgh, he took responsibility for the building of the Chapel of St Albert the Great. The process drew upon the knowledge and expertise of skilled professionals within the congregation to create a new church which deservedly won its place among the top hundred in *Scotstyle* 2016.

Chapel of St Albert the Great, Edinburgh –Simpson & Brown Architects, 2012 © Chris Humphreys

" In the late light of a winter's day, it can seem as if our chapel was once no more than a garden wall but that then some kindly hand had unfurled a canopy of oak for shelter, resting it in the branches of four bare trees. At first light, you can almost believe that the hidden hand might roll back the canopy, and slide away the side wall, opening the space to the sky and the sun. With this gentle magic, stillness and movement continually embrace the light of the coming day.

With thanks to RIAS for honouring this alchemy of steel, stone, wood, glass and light.

With best wishes in this centenary year,

"

Dr Donnie Munro Hon FRIAS

A NATIVE GAELIC SPEAKER, born in Uig, Isle of Skye, Donnie was educated at Portree High School where he first encountered his Runrig colleagues. He subsequently took a degree in Fine Arts and completed his post-graduate education studies in Edinburgh (and recorded his first Runrig album). He taught in Inverness and Edinburgh.

Runrig turned professional in 1982, producing a series of highly acclaimed Celtic Rock albums. International success followed.

Munro was elected Rector of the University of Edinburgh in 1991. He became a Trustee with Sabhal Mòr Ostaig the Gaelic College in Skye and subsequently Director of Development, Fundraising and the Arts. He has served in high profile roles in the promotion of Gaelic arts and culture and is a successful solo artist, writer and performer.

" I am deeply honoured to have been appointed as an Honorary FRIAS in this very special year and deeply appreciative of having had the opportunity, over recent years, of working professionally with some of Scotland's most innovative architects, on a range of exciting projects both on my home island of Skye and on the island of Islay.

As someone whose professional training was in the field of visual arts and design, I have long been deeply aware of the uniquely privileged opportunity which architects have, as artists, to make important public works which impact profoundly on all our all our lives and visual statements which remain for many years an important feature of our shared material culture and our environment, both urban and rural.

I congratulate the RIAS and all its members on this year of celebration.

'Still-life West Coast Window' acrylic on canvas

John Norman Hon FRIAS

BROUGHT UP IN EDINBURGH in the 1950s and Dublin in the 1960s, John was educated at Catholic boarding school in England and studied Mathematics at Trinity College Dublin. He moved back to Edinburgh and worked in insurance "for a wee bit". He then spent a year out, working with the homeless in Glasgow and then as an assistant at an Edinburgh church.

John obtained his diploma in accounting from Heriot Watt and qualified as a CA, subsequently setting up in partnership and with a speciality in charity accounts. He first worked with the RIAS in the 1980s and has done a brilliant job as the Incorporation's accountant since 2008.

" I congratulate the RIAS on the occasion of its attaining 100 years.

I have been associated in various ways with the accountancy function of the RIAS for over 30 of those years, since being part of the audit team in the early 1980's to my present function as the consultant accountant. I thought it might be of interest to compare the accounts of 100 years ago of the 'Institute of Scottish Architects' (as it was then) with the accounts today and to note some other financial facts from those early days. For this I have had access to the beautifully bound minutes of the Incorporation, which have just been returned from the bookbinder to preserve this invaluable record for posterity.

The most recent RIAS accounts for the year 2015 run to 26 pages and show a turnover of £1.4 million. By contrast the first accounts of the 'Institute', covering the period 21 November 1916 to 31 December 1918, are contained on a single sheet of foolscap and show income of just £552. They also show generous endowments from the founding father of the Institute, Sir Robert Rowand Anderson, of £5,000 to be retained as capital in the ordinary fund and £500 to set up a benevolent fund. The capital was invested in 5% War Stock 1929-47 to provide a steady source of annual income.

Annual membership dues, first charged for the year 1918, were five shillings for Fellows, two shillings and sixpence for Associates and one shilling for students. No dues were charged for members on active war service. The total dues for 1918 came to £60 11/-, when the membership numbered 353.

The first Secretary and Treasurer, W.G. Walker C.A. was paid an annual salary of £50 in 1917-18. The audit fee paid to James Walker C.A. (presumably no relation) was £5. The audit report was a two-liner compared to the two pages of today. Such is the spread of regulation!

A rent of seven shillings & sixpence was paid to the Edinburgh Architectural Association for each Council meeting held in their premises at 117 George St. Travel expenses for attendance at meetings were reimbursed at half of the 1st class rail fare.

The application for a royal charter, which was granted on 6th May 1922, cost £500. This followed an agreed name change to the 'Incorporation of Architects in Scotland' so as not to be confused with the existing 'Royal Institute of British Architecture' (RIBA), which was UK wide. Later that year the RIAS was recognised as a charity and no longer had to pay income tax of 5/- in the £ on interest.

The accounts for 1922 record a generous legacy payment of £18,000 from the estate of Rowand Anderson, who died in 1921, aged 87, just a few months after his wife. The minutes record that under his will he also bequeathed his house at 15 Rutland Square "to form, as expressly stated in the Donor's testament, a permanent home for the Institute". All this ensured that the RIAS started life on a very sound financial footing and of course 15 Rutland Square remains in occupation as its headquarters to this day.

There is an interesting parallel here with my own Institute of Chartered Accountants of Scotland (ICAS), which was also housed in former residential properties in the New Town of Edinburgh, from 1891 to 2000, initially at 27 Queen Street and latterly in 4 adjacent properties at 26 to 29 Queen Street. It may be noted that in the initial alterations of 1891 to No. 27, the entire second floor was given over to a billiard room and a smoking room, which perhaps says something about professional priorities in those days! ICAS moved to new purpose built headquarters in 2000, while a similar move proposed for the RIAS was decided against – no doubt under the approving eye of Sir Robert.

By a strange co-incidence the day that I was consulting the minutes, 1st June 1916, turned out to be the 95th anniversary date of the death of Sir Rowand Anderson in 1921. "

Sources:
Council minutes of the Royal Incorporation of Architects in Scotland.
'Twenty Seven Queen Street, Edinburgh – Home of Scottish Chartered Accountants 1891 – 2000' by Sam McKinstry.

Ian Rankin OBE Hon FRIAS

BORN IN THE KINGDOM OF FIFE in 1960, Ian Rankin graduated from the University of Edinburgh in 1982, and then spent three years writing novels when he was supposed to be working towards a PhD in Scottish Literature.

Ian Rankin started his writing life as a poet but didn't get very far. Ian is the creator of Inspector Rebus. The Rebus novels are international best sellers, translated into more than thirty languages.

Ian has received an OBE for services to literature, opting to receive the prize in his home city of Edinburgh, where he lives with his wife and two sons.

Writing about music is like dancing about architecture…

Architecture is a waltz,

a two-step,

an arabesque

To a soundtrack of Form
Space
and Function,

Its perfume heady as jazz and geometry,
On a dancefloor the width of our imagination,

While movements deft
And sinuous
Wrap themselves
Around us,

Partnering and beguiling,
Beguiling and partnering,
Partnering and beguilding,

Making dancers of us all.

Ian Ritchie CBE Hon FRIAS

IAN RITCHIE IS A DIRECTOR of Ian Ritchie Architects, a Royal Academician and an elected member of the Akademie der Künste. He is the Special Visiting Professor of Architecture at Liverpool University; he advises The Ove Arup Foundation, is Dean of Architecture at the University of Greenwich, a trustee of the Backstage Trust and a Governor of the RSC.

Ian has chaired many international juries, including the RIAS Doolan Award and RIBA Stirling Prize. His practice has received more than 60 major national and international awards. He has written several books and his art is held in international galleries and museums.

Design CTST VAN RITCHIE 1 Printed by ScotWeave \\DESIGN3-PC\Epson Stylus Phot (720 dpi) Mon. 2nd May. 2016 12:04
Folder : Y:\Scotweave\Dobby\Design\LCP\Geoffrey (Tailor) Warp [A] 40.00 ends/inch Milled : 2 Weft Ratio : 50%
Weft [A] 40.00 picks/inch T16vm m0 f100 c-1x-1 wx0 fx0 s0 0 0

Warp yarns

HAPPY CENTENARY BIRTHDAY
TO THE RIAS
I've designed a new family tartan
to celebrate it.

83

Dr Alastair Ross Hon FRIAS

BORN IN PERTH IN 1941, the sculptor Alastair Ross studied at Duncan of Jordanstone College of Art, Dundee, then in Vienna, Rome and Athens on a post-graduate scholarship. In his early years as a student the Florentine renaissance master Donatello was a major influence, as was the Croatian sculptor Ivan Mestrovic along with the German sculptor Wilhelm Lehmbruck and Fritz Wotruba from Vienna.

However in Ross' personal pantheon of sculptural heroes, one artist above all others was, and remains, of seminal influence in his development as an artist – namely Auguste Rodin the nineteenth century French master.

Alastair R. Ross.

Alastair Salvesen CBE Hon FRIAS

BORN IN 1941, ALASTAIR SALVESEN has supported the Dovecot Studios for many years and was the most substantial private donor for its relocation to Infirmary Street. Since 1989 he has supported a travelling scholarship for Scotland's best young artist and in 1992 gifted a new, purpose-built, organ to St. Giles' Cathedral, Edinburgh.

Alastair has been Chairman of Dawnfresh Seafoods Ltd since 1983, Chairman of Archangels Informal Investment Ltd since 2009, President of the Royal Highland & Agricultural Society of Scotland (2001-02), member of the Council for the Royal Society of Arts from 2005, Governor of the Fettes Trust since 1994 and Governor of the Donaldson's Trust (1997-2009). He is a member of the Queen's Bodyguard for Scotland and received the Queen's Jubilee Medal.

“ Art for architecture

I and The Dovecot Foundation are proud to support another fine creative institution in Scotland. The Dovecot Tapestry Studio, based in the former Infirmary Street Baths in Edinburgh, is Scotland's only tapestry studios. Originally established in 1912, Dovecot weaves magic with some of the world's most remarkable artists, often in collaboration with architects, whose vision for art integrated into their architecture we so enjoy and admire.

Many Happy Returns RIAS, and may your architects continue that fine tradition of commissioning art for architecture – and particularly woven art – for many years to come … ”

Dr Ken Shuttleworth Hon FRIAS

KEN SHUTTLEWORTH STUDIED architecture at the Leicester School of Architecture, where his fluid draftsmanship earned him the nickname "Ken the Pen". As a partner at Foster and Partners he worked on some of the world's most iconic buildings. From 1979 he oversaw The Hong Kong and Shanghai Banking Corporation's headquarters project. Back in the UK from 1986, he built up a remarkable portfolio of projects.

Shuttleworth set up his own practice, Make Architects, in 2004. They have completed numerous award-winning buildings, including the City of London Information Centre, Grosvenor Waterside and 10 Weymouth Street residential schemes. Other UK projects include The Cube in Birmingham and the Handball Arena for the London 2012 Olympics, 'the Copper Box'.

Ken was a CABE commissioner from 2004–2011.

making the best . . .

" . . . achieving the best is not about off-the-shelf . solutions or formulaic processes . Its about having the curiosity to explore the unique + full potential of every opportunity . . . "

Ken Shuttleworth
make architects

Lord Chris Smith Hon FRIAS

CHRIS SMITH GREW UP in Edinburgh. He was Labour MP for Islington South & Finsbury, 1983-2005 and Secretary of State for Culture, Media and Sport 1997-2001. Smith created CABE, provided free admission to national museums, and promoted the creative industries. He led parliamentary opposition to the Iraq war in 2003.

Smith was founding Director of the Clore Leadership Programme for future leaders in the arts and culture; Chairman of the Environment Agency 2008-2014; Chairman of the Advertising Standards Authority since 2007; and is now Master of Pembroke College Cambridge.

Dear Royal Incorporation of Architects in Scotland,

Many congratulations on reaching — and celebrating — your centenary. Scotland has always been a country of true creativity, and nowhere has this been more true than in architecture. From the glorious heritage of the past to the exciting innovation of the present, our built environment, the way it meets and complements the landscape, our cityscapes and rural locations: there is so much for us to be proud of. And the RIAS has been at the heart of it all.

Thank you!

Chris Smith

Professor Steven Spier Hon FRIAS

PROFESSOR STEVEN SPIER HAS BEEN Dean of the Faculty of Art, Design and Architecture at Kingston University London since September 2012. Born in Montreal, he grew up in the USA and has a BA in philosophy and a Master of Architecture from SCI-Arc in Los Angeles.

Previously head of the School of Architecture and Design in Belfast, founding Vice-Chancellor of the HafenCity University Hamburg and head of the Strathclyde University School of Architecture, he is author of the influential *Swiss Made*, as well as numerous academic articles.

Steven is currently on the board of Cryptic Glasgow. He was a director of Scottish Ballet 2003-12, and a director on the first board of Architecture and Design Scotland.

" 'I knew that architecture was made possible by the confrontation of a precise form with time and the elements, a confrontation which lasted until the form was destroyed in the process of this combat. Architecture was one of the ways that humanity has sought to survive; it was a way of expressing the fundamental search for happiness.'

From Aldo Rossi's *A Scientific Autobiography*, 1981

Happy Birthday RIAS, and many more. "

Dr Gavin Stamp Hon FRIAS

GAVIN STAMP IS AN ARCHITECTURAL historian and writer. Born in Kent in 1948, he taught the history of architecture at the Mackintosh School of Architecture, at the invitation of the late Professor Andy MacMillan, from 1990 until 2003, during which time he founded the Alexander Thomson Society and, with Murray Grigor, organised the 1999 exhibition about the great Glasgow designer.

Amongst Scottish architects and architects who worked in Scotland, Stamp has written about Mackintosh, JJ Burnet, Eugene Bourdon, Robert Weir Schultz, George and Giles Gilbert Scott, Edwin Lutyens, John Soane, Gillespie, Kidd & Coia, and, of course, Greek Thomson.

" RIAS@100:

congratulations and thanks from a proud foreign Hon. Fellow

To celebrate the centenary of the RIAS I offer a photograph of a design by Glasgow's – and Scotland's – greatest Victorian architect, but one that is unusual and rare because it is in England. It is one of two cast-iron lamp-posts-cum-ventilation-shafts still to be found in New Cross in South-East London. This model was chosen, presumably, from the catalogue of the products of the Saracen Foundry of Walter Macfarlane & Co.. The prototype was designed by Alexander 'Greek' Thomson as one of six that once stood in Union Street outside his Egyptian Halls. Today, all trace of that great iron-foundry business has disappeared from Glasgow while – to Scotland's shame – Thomson's finest commercial building is in a perilous state of decay. Perhaps, to mark this centenary, something should be done at long last about Egyptian Halls, a magnificent work by one of Scotland's most original architectural talents and greatest minds. "

Daphne Thissen Hon FRIAS

DAPHNE THISSEN'S PROFESSOR AT the University of Groningen inspired her to study Architectural History and planted the seed of her continuing interest in contemporary Western European architecture. After completing her MA, she worked for the architecture research team at English Heritage in Cambridge, before being appointed as Cultural Attaché at the Embassy of the Kingdom of the Netherlands in London.

In her current role, Daphne is responsible for strengthening professional and cultural architectural relations. She has a particular interest in Scotland and Scottish contemporary architecture inspired by her contact with RIAS and twice participating in the Doolan Prize jury.

"This beautiful painting of a Dutch winter landscape, part of the Scottish National collection, really emphasises the Scottish-Dutch connection for me; showing normal life in a beautiful setting, very much like Scottish painters do. In my day to day work I regularly speak with both Dutch and Scottish artists, architects and other creative individuals who all say they love working with each other – I like to think this is because we 'get' each other.

Both nationals tell me they find comfort in the similar way of doing business, straightforward and to the point, the recognisable sense of humour, pretty straightforward as well, and the various language connections (although in my experience less Dutch people are aware of those than the Scots are).

For me, the most striking difference is in the landscape (as illustrated in the picture – the Netherlands still has endless horizons and skies) and the site specific architecture. I am personally very much in awe of the breath-taking Scottish landscapes and the way Scottish architects design buildings that make full use of what is naturally on offer."

Salomon van Ruysdael, "Alkmaar in Winter" © Scottish National Gallery

Patrick Tyler Hon FRIAS

NOW RETIRED AFTER 44 YEARS in insurance, the highlight of Patrick's challenging career was the setting up of RIAS Insurance Services in 1984. That endeavour brought him from London on a two-year contract. He never returned, and has adopted the wonderful city of Edinburgh as home!

Born in London, early years in Switzerland and Liverpool, and many a foreign holiday, all fostered a passion for local history and culture. He has a particular interest in the Mansfield Traquair Centre (and involvement as a Friend). This once-abandoned, Rowand Anderson church, has been rescued and given new life for the 21st century.

" Three cheers to the RIAS for a wonderful 100th anniversary

I had over 25 years' involvement with the RIAS, being a one-time Managing Director of RIAS Insurance Services – a company born of the inspiration of my good friend, Charles McKean.

We were a unique and committed team of Architects and Insurers. The company was set up in 1984 and, after only 5 years in business, we were privileged to provide insurance cover to over 80% of all RIAS practices.

It was an adventure I enjoyed on many levels – building up the business, visiting practices in all corners of the country, discussing with RIAS members their projects, problems and successes, coping with change and, of course, joining in the annual Convention parties.

It was a huge pleasure to work with and get to know so many RIAS members and staff, past and present.

A happy birthday to you all!

Professor David Walker Hon FRIAS

PROFESSOR DAVID WALKER IS A product of Dundee College of Art – as it then was – and joined the Scottish Office as a historic buildings investigator in 1961, retiring as Chief Inspector of Historic Buildings in 1993.

Between 1994 and 2001 David taught architectural history at the University of St Andrews. From 2002 until 2007 he was founder-editor of the online Dictionary of Scottish Architects 1840-1940, consolidating and greatly augmenting his research begun in the 1950s.

From the early 1980s David worked closely with the late Professor Charles McKean on the RIAS Guides, co-authoring those for Edinburgh and Dundee.

" Remembering Annie Anderson

In the south-eastern area of Warriston Cemetery, not far from where I write, there is a small but beautifully detailed and lettered gothic gravestone. At its head is a quatrefoil, hollowed out to shelter an alto-relievo of Christ with a little girl and a lamb. It was erected to commemorate the short life of Annie Ross Anderson who died of typhoid at the age of eight on 14 February 1872. The story of her illness and death is movingly told in her father's own words in Professor Sam McKinstry's *Rowand Anderson: the Premier Architect of Scotland*.

What, you may ask, has Annie to do with the RIAS? While the professional associations in the Scottish cities had been discussing the re-establishment of their lapsed Architectural Institute of Scotland since 1897 and would doubtless have come together again eventually, the short answer is everything. Annie was her parents' only child. Probably driven by the pain of her loss, Anderson made a determined attempt to win the competition for Edinburgh University's new Medical School and Graduation Hall in 1874-75, undertaking a hugely expensive study tour of comparable buildings in England, The Netherlands, France and Germany to master every aspect of the brief.

He was a deserving winner. His elevations in a North Italian Early Renaissance style were supremely well composed from every angle and were plainly intended to excel Sir George Gilbert Scott's new University in Glasgow in quality if not quite in extent. There is, so far as I know, no record of Anderson making a further study tour in and around Venice, but the sheer quality of detail in the executed buildings suggests that he must have done. His architecture was completely novel at the time, a triumph of the academic side of the Aesthetic Movement, and as Sir John Summerson acknowledged some thirty years ago, it had no counterpart in the contemporary architecture of London. Even without its St Marks'-inspired campanile – actually the ventilation tower – which would have made the challenge to Glasgow University all the more telling, it remains the finest thing that Anderson ever built. It left the architects of the previous generation looking just a little old-fashioned and laid the foundation of a practice which brought him greater wealth than any other Scottish architect of his generation.

In his fifties Anderson began to consider the causes to which that wealth might be devoted. By 1889 he had been elected President of the architectural section of the National Association for the Advancement of Art and its Application to Industry. The Association's meeting that year was held in Anderson's newly-completed Scottish National Portrait Gallery, the supreme embodiment of his belief that there was only one art and that Post-Renaissance distinctions between Fine Art and the useful arts were artificial and unhelpful. All of the lecturers were carefully chosen to make the case for Anderson's planned School of Applied Art embracing Architecture, Decoration, Sculpture and Wood-carving, Metal-working, Glass-staining, Cabinet-making and Printing and Bookbinding. With the support of the Board of Manufactures, the Town Council and thirty other subscribers the School of Applied Art opened in what is now the Royal Scottish Academy in October 1892, Anderson visiting London and Paris to acquire high-quality casts, photographs and books which cost him £400. That might not seem a lot now but at the time it was enough to build a good-quality semi-detached house. The School of Applied Art transformed the teaching of architecture in Scotland, particularly in the period up to 1897 when the École des Beaux Arts-trained Frank Simon and Stewart Henbest Capper were in charge and presented the students with a real intellectual challenge.

Finally, as every member of the RIAS knows, Anderson effectively founded the Incorporation with a gift of £5,000 in 1916. On his death in 1921 he bequeathed his house at 15 Rutland Square and the residue of his estate – £69,787 – to ensure that the Incorporation would not wither as its predecessor, the Architectural Institute, had done. As Anderson had anticipated, the Incorporation received its Royal Charter in 1922.

But if Annie had lived, and there had been grandchildren to provide for, the Incorporation would not be where it is, might not have come into existence until much later, and might never have possessed its own premises. Give Annie and her parents a thought, and perhaps even a visit now that the Friends of Warriston Cemetery have tidied the place up and compiled studies of its sculpture. "

Kirsty Wark Hon FRIAS

ONE OF BRITAIN'S MOST EXPERIENCED television journalists, Kirsty was born in Dumfries and educated in Kilmarnock. She has presented a wide range of programmes - from the ground breaking *Late Show* to Election specials, live stadium events and, since 1993, the BBC's flagship nightly current affairs show *Newsnight*. She has conducted long form interviews with everyone from Margaret Thatcher to Madonna.

Kirsty has made cameo appearances in a wide range of television dramas, radio programmes and films. She reached the final in *Celebrity Masterchef* in 2011 and hosted the culinary quiz *A Question of Taste* for BBC2.

Kirsty has won several major awards, including three BAFTA Awards. Her debut novel, *The Legacy of Elizabeth Pringle*, was published in March 2014.

100

R.I.A.S.

Professor Ian Wall Hon FRIAS

PROFESSOR WALL TEACHES AT BOTH Heriot-Watt University and Aberdeen's Scott Sutherland School. A former Chief Executive of EDI, Edinburgh Council's property development company, Ian was responsible for EDI's initial project – the commissioning of Edinburgh Park. At EDI, he oversaw the delivery of tens of thousands of square metres of industrial spaces and numerous award-winning residential developments. In 2001, 2002, 2003 and 2004 he was recognised by the RIBA as one of Britain's best clients.

Ian's many enthusiasms include the Edinburgh International Science Festival, which he invented, the International Centre for Mathematical Sciences, WASPS, a charitable landlord for over 400 artists, Wester Hailes Land and Property Trust, The Scottish Poetry Library, which he also Chairs and The Royal Botanic Gardens in Edinburgh where he is a Trustee.

Ian White Hon FRIAS

IAN FOUNDED IAN WHITE ASSOCIATES in 1974 and is now a consultant to the practice. Major projects included the Scottish Exhibition and Conference Centre, Dundee Technology Park, Glasgow Cathedral Precinct and Edinburgh Park. Ian acted as Advisor to the Forestry Commission and as landscape consultant to London Docklands, The National Trust, Scotland's National Galleries and National Museums, Scottish Enterprise, The University of Dundee and many local authorities. He has extensive experience in the conservation of designed landscapes and the settings of listed buildings.

Ian is a Fellow of the Landscape Institute, has taught at Glasgow School of Art, Heriot-Watt and Robert Gordon Universities and served as an external examiner. A past Honorary Secretary of the Landscape Institute he is past Chairman of the Landscape Institute, Scotland.

Edinburgh Park celebrates design where ordered site planning, landscape design and architecture combine to create a distinct new element in the city which can be discovered and enjoyed by workers, visitors, swans and ducks.

New Edinburgh : Ian Wall *HonFRIAS*
Masterplanner : Richard Meier *HonFRIAS*
Architect : Ian Arbott *FRIAS*
Landscape Architect : Ian White *HonFRIAS*

Adrian Wiszniewski Hon FRIAS

BORN IN GLASGOW, ADRIAN STUDIED architecture at the Mackintosh School and then attended Glasgow School of Art. He belongs to the group known as 'The New Glasgow Boys' who led the revival of figurative painting in Scottish art during the 1980s.

Wiszniewski has worked in neon, tapestry, painting and sculpture, ceramics and printmaking. He won the competition for the David Dale gateway to Glasgow Green with a mural of galvanised steel sculpted heads, which somehow still conveys the dream-like quality of much of his art. He has collaborated on several architectural projects. His work features in major public collections including MOMA New York, Tate, London and Setegaya, Tokyo. He has had around 50 solo exhibitions throughout the world.

School of Architecture - auscneuses.

RIAS Honorary Fellows

Mr Robert Adam Hon FRIAS

Mr Charles Anderson Hon FRIAS

Mr Peter Anderson Hon FRIAS

Mr Tadao Ando Hon FRIAS

Rt Hon Lord Balfour of Burleigh Hon FRIAS

Mr Oliver Barratt MBE Hon FRIAS

Mr Neil Baxter Hon FRIAS

Mr Mark Beaumont Hon FRIAS

Mr Louis Becker Hon FRIAS

Dame Elizabeth Blackadder Hon FRIAS

Ms Angela Brady OBE PPRIBA Hon FRIAS

Mr George Burnet Hon FRIAS

Sir Henry (Harry) Burns Hon FRIAS

Dr John Byrne Hon FRIAS

Dr Santiago Calatrava Hon FRIAS

Mr Joan Callis Hon FRIAS

Sir Kenneth Calman Hon FRIAS

Rt Hon Lord Cameron of Lochbroom Hon FRIAS

Mr Stuart Campbell Hon FRIAS

Mr Douglas Cardinal Hon FRIAS

Mr Richard Carr Hon FRIAS

Mrs Patricia Chalmers MBE Hon FRIAS

Sir Sean Connery Hon FRIAS

Mr David Cook Hon FRIAS

Dr Malcolm Cooper Hon FRIAS

Mr Edward Cullinan CBE Hon FRIAS

Mrs Kathleen Dalyell OBE Hon FRIAS

Mr Tam Dalyell Hon FRIAS

Ms Elizabeth Davidson OBE Hon FRIAS

Mr Richard Demarco OBE Hon FRIAS

Mrs Margaret Doolan Hon FRIAS

Mr Patrick Doyle Hon FRIAS

HRH Prince Philip Duke of Edinburgh Hon FRIAS

HRH Duke of Gloucester GCVO Hon FRIAS

Mr John Dunbar OBE Hon FRIAS

Sir Robin Duthie CBE Hon FRIAS

Mr Hugh Dutton Hon FRIAS

Mr Joachim Eble Hon FRIAS

Mr Christophe Egret Hon FRIAS

Mr Marc Ellington Hon FRIAS

Ms Linda Fabiani Hon FRIAS

Sir Terry Farrell Hon FRIAS

Mr George Ferguson CBE PPRIBA Hon FRIAS

Mr Paul Finch OBE Hon FRIAS

Professor Magnus Fladmark Hon FRIAS

Lord Norman Foster Hon FRIAS

Dr John Frew Hon FRIAS

Mr Mike Galloway OBE Hon FRIAS

Professor Jan Gehl Hon FRIAS

Mr Clive Gillman Hon FRIAS

Dame Evelyn Glennie Hon FRIAS

Ms Annabel Goldie Hon FRIAS

Mr Edgar Gonzalez Hon FRIAS

Mrs Maureen Goodfellow Hon FRIAS

Mr Piers Gough CBE Hon FRIAS

Mr Ian Gow Hon FRIAS

Ms Muriel Gray Hon FRIAS

Sir Paul Grice Hon FRIAS

Mr Murray Grigor Hon FRIAS

Sir Nicholas Grimshaw CBE Hon FRIAS

Sir Angus Grossart CBE Hon FRIAS

Mr Robin Harper Hon FRIAS

Mr Patrick Harrison CBE Hon FRIAS

Professor Herman Hertzberger Hon FRIAS

Professor Peter Higgs Hon FRIAS

Ms Patricia Hopkins Hon FRIAS

Sir Michael Hopkins CBE Hon FRIAS

Professor Malcolm Horner Hon FRIAS

Professor John Hume OBE Hon FRIAS

Mr Ronald Jamieson MBE Hon FRIAS

Mr Charles Jencks Hon FRIAS

Ms Eva Jiřičná CBE Hon FRIAS

Mr Rob Joiner Hon FRIAS

Mr Alan Jones PPRSUA Hon FRIAS

Mme Nathalie Regnier Kagan Hon FRIAS

Dame Barbara Kelly Hon FRIAS

Mr Neil Kelly Hon FRIAS

Professor Martin Kemp Hon FRIAS

Professor Hiroaki Kimura Hon FRIAS

Mr Stefan King Hon FRIAS

Mr Brian Knox Hon FRIAS

Professor Rob Krier Hon FRIAS

Mr Patrick Lally Hon FRIAS

Mrs Lorraine Landels Hon FRIAS

Mr Henning Larsen Hon FRIAS

Dr Eusebio Leal Spengler Hon FRIAS

Ms Liz Lochhead Hon FRIAS

Ms Phyllis Logan Hon FRIAS

Dr Anne Lorne Gillies Hon FRIAS

Professor Michael Lynch Hon FRIAS

Mr Thomas Macartney Hon FRIAS

Dr James Macaulay Hon FRIAS

Mr Tim Macfarlane Hon FRIAS

Lord Macfarlane of Bearsden KT Hon FRIAS

Lord MacLennan of Rogart Hon FRIAS

Mrs Angela MacMillan Hon FRIAS

Sir James MacMillan CBE Hon FRIAS

Ms Sally Magnusson Hon FRIAS

Mr Fumihiko Maki Hon FRIAS

President Pasqual Maragall Hon FRIAS

Mr Roy Martin Hon FRIAS

Mr Alan Massie Hon FRIAS

Professor Tom Maver Hon FRIAS

Ms Eleanor McAllister OBE Hon FRIAS

Mr Ian McCallum Hon FRIAS

Ms Anne McChlery Hon FRIAS

Mr Jim McColl MBE Hon FRIAS

Ms Val McDermid Hon FRIAS

Dr Lori McElroy MBE Hon FRIAS

Mr Tom McInally Hon FRIAS

Ms Suzanne McIntosh Hon FRIAS

Mr Richard Meier Hon FRIAS

Mrs Dany Metzstein Hon FRIAS

Mr Bruce Minto Hon FRIAS

Mr Rafael Moneo Valles Hon FRIAS

Mr Brian Moore Hon FRIAS

Fr Dermot Morrin Hon FRIAS

Dr Donnie Munro Hon FRIAS

Mr Glenn Murcutt Hon FRIAS

Mr David Narro Hon FRIAS

Mr John Norman Hon FRIAS

Mrs Ann Packard Hon FRIAS

Mr Bill Paterson Hon FRIAS

Professor Renzo Piano Hon FRIAS

Mr Sunand Prasad PPRIBA Hon FRIAS

Mr Charles Prosser Hon FRIAS

Mr Ian Rankin OBE Hon FRIAS

Ms Ruth Reed PPRIBA Hon FRIAS

Mr Gordon Reid Hon FRIAS

Mr Reto Renggli Hon FRIAS

Mr Ian Ritchie CBE Hon FRIAS

Lord Richard Rogers Hon FRIAS

Dr Alastair Ross Hon FRIAS

Professor Alistair Rowan Hon FRIAS

Professor Tina Saaby Madsen Hon FRIAS

Mr Moshe Safdie Hon FRIAS

Mr Alastair Salvesen CBE Hon FRIAS

Mr Andy Scott Hon FRIAS

Mr Tavish Scott Hon FRIAS

Ms Mia Scott Hon FRIAS

Dr Ken Shuttleworth Hon FRIAS

Professor Mona Siddiqui OBE Hon FRIAS

Mr Alvaro Siza Hon FRIAS

Professor Vladimir Slapeta Hon FRIAS

Dr Tommy Smith Hon FRIAS

Lord Chris Smith Hon FRIAS

Professor Sean Smith Hon FRIAS

Professor Steven Spier Hon FRIAS

Dr Gavin Stamp Hon FRIAS

Mr Phillippe Starck Hon FRIAS

Mr Brian Stewart Hon FRIAS

Mr Deyan Sudjic OBE Hon FRIAS

Ms Benedetta Tagliabue Hon FRIAS

Ms Daphne Thissen Hon FRIAS

Mr Patrick Tyler Hon FRIAS

Mr Robert Venturi Hon FRIAS

Professor David Walker Hon FRIAS

Professor Ian Wall Hon FRIAS

Ms Kirsty Wark Hon FRIAS

Mr Albert Watson OBE Hon FRIAS

Mr Gordon Watson Hon FRIAS

Ms Karyn Watt Hon FRIAS

Mr Ian White Hon FRIAS

Mr Bob Winter Hon FRIAS

Mrs Ruth Wishart Hon FRIAS

Mr Adrian Wiszniewski Hon FRIAS

Lady Sarah Wolffe Hon FRIAS

The Rt Hon James Wolffe Hon FRIAS

Dr Kenneth Yeang Hon FRIAS

Acknowledgements

THE INCORPORATION IS VERY GRATEFUL to Liz Lochhead Hon FRIAS for her help in promoting and gathering the content of this book. We are also grateful to all of the Honorary Fellows of the Incorporation who have submitted their poems, prose, thoughts, doodles, drawings, paintings and photographs to this 100th birthday card.

The RIAS' Honorary Fellows enhance the standing and reach of Scotland's professional body for architects. They also reinforce the message that good buildings improve health, wellbeing, social cohesion and can even add fun to our everyday lives – for that we are grateful to all our Honorary Fellows, at home and overseas.

The editor would like to extend a further personal thank you to Liz Lochhead for her help and generous support. He also wishes to thank Carol-Ann Hildersley, without whom nothing would get done and Jon Jardine for being such a brilliant graphic designer and a pal. A message of special thanks also to Josh McGuire and Lily Baxter-McGuire.